7601

WHOSE NOSE
IS THIS?

JOANNE RANDOLPH

PowerKiDS press™

New York

Published in 2009 by The Rosen Publishing Group, Inc.
29 East 21st Street, New York, NY 10010

First Edition

Book Design: Julio Gil
Photo Researcher: Jessica Gerweck

Photo Credits: All images from Shutterstock.com.

Library of Congress Cataloging-in-Publication Data

Randolph, Joanne.
  Whose nose is this? / Joanne Randolph. — 1st ed.
     p. cm. — (Animal clues)
  Includes index.
  ISBN 978-1-4042-4451-1 (library binding)
  1. Nose—Juvenile literature. I. Title.
  QL947.R35 2009
  590—dc22
                                              2007048203

Manufactured in the United States of America

CONTENTS

Whose nose is long and gray?

An elephant's nose is long and gray.

Whose nose is black and **round**?

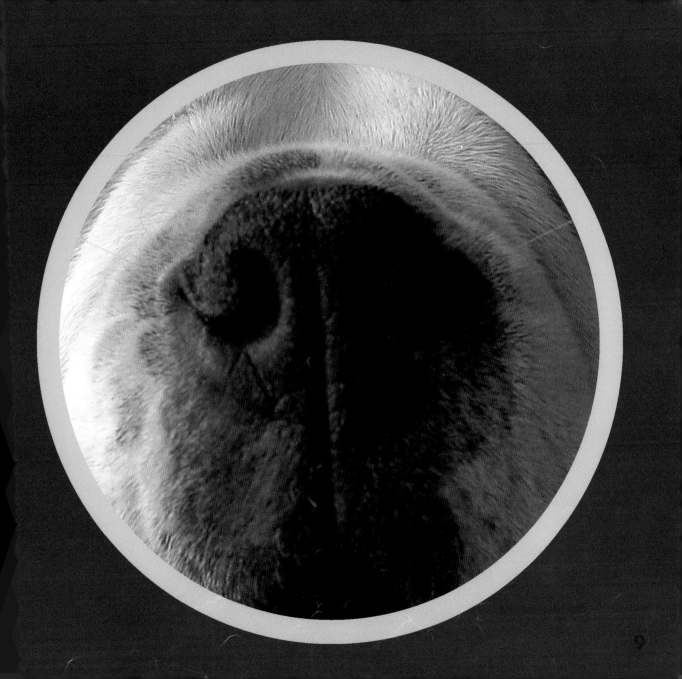

This bulldog's nose is black and round.

Which animal has a nose with two **pointy horns**?

13

A rhino has a nose with two pointy horns.

Whose nose is this, with its funny **folds**?

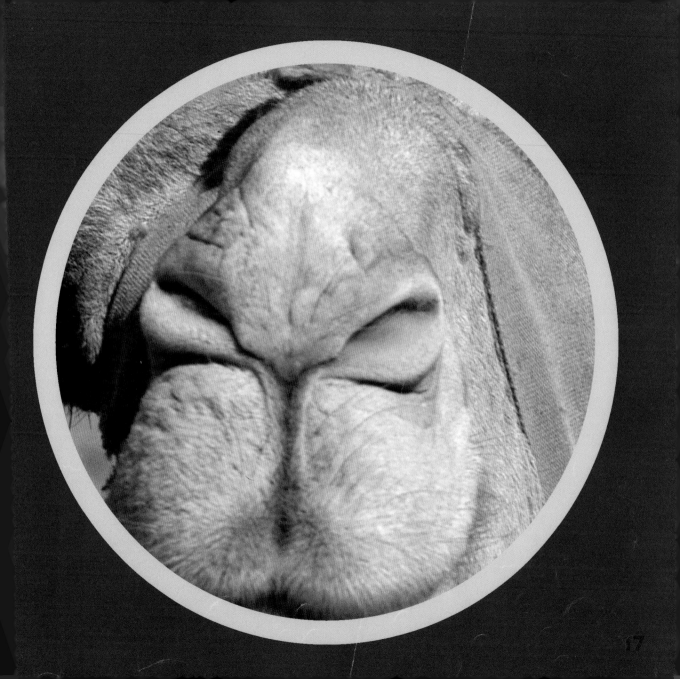
17

A camel belongs to this nose with the funny folds.

Whose nose has holes that sit on top?

21

A hippo's nose has holes that sit on top.

WORDS TO KNOW

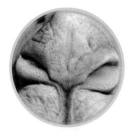

folds

horns

pointy

round

INDEX

WEB SITES

Due to the changing nature of Internet links, PowerKids Press has developed an online list of Web sites related to the subject of this book. This site is updated regularly. Please use this link to access the list:
www.powerkidslinks.com/acl/nose/

24